Summary of

The Complete Guide to Fasting:

Heal Your Body Through Intermittent,

Alternate-Day, and Extended Fasting

D1710911

Written by

Jason Fung, MD

&

Jimmy Moore

Summarized by Brief Books

Note to readers:

This is an unofficial summary & analysis of *The Complete Guide to Fasting: Heal Your Body Through Intermittent, Alternate-Day, and Extended Fasting* by Jason Fung, MD, and Jimmy Moore. It is designed to enrich your reading experience. We encourage you to purchase the original book.

Table of Contents

Book Summary

The Complete Guide to Fasting: Heal Your Body Through Intermittent, Alternate-Day, and Extended Fasting

This book is an incredibly fascinating read, particularly for anyone who is obese or has type 2 diabetes. Each "theory" is supported by studies and references making the terms and solutions very believable and easy to follow.

Fasting is indeed a viable option for losing weight and reversing a type 2 diabetes diagnosis. You will experience lowered blood pressure, blood sugar, cholesterol and greater energy and brain power.

The book exposes you to real life examples of highly successful fasting experiences and the fasting all stars that accomplished it. *The Complete Guide to Fasting: Heal Your Body Through Intermittent, Alternate-Day, and Extended Fasting* is a thought provoking piece of work that presents the open mind with great insight that is very different from what most of us have traditionally been taught to believe and understand.

I would also recommend this book for individuals who practice medicine because the information provided is very different from what most patients are "taught" during their lives. Whether you want to agree with the reported findings or not is certainly your own discretion.

Character List

The Complete Guide to Fasting: Heal Your Body Through Intermittent, Alternate-Day, and Extended Fasting

NOTE: All characters are used as examples only. The book is not a novel, rather an instructional book and this list is intended to help the reader remember the cases associated with the stories. This group of individuals is called "Fasting All Stars."

Abel James is another best-selling author and hosts the *Fat Burning Man* podcasts. In 2015 and 2016, he was named one of the 100 most influential people in health and fitness by Greatist. He is also a noted orator, song writer, and instrumentalist. **Fatburningman.com**

Amy Berger, MS, CNS, NTP is also an author and has a Master's Degree in human nutrition. She is a former US Air Force veteran and has a keen interest in low carb for neurological health, including traumatic brain injury. She is now dedicated to helping others better understand nutrition and physiology. **Tuitnutrition.com**

Dr. Richard Ruscio helps people nationwide using lab based natural medicine treatments.
Drruscio.com

Dr. Bert Herring is a pioneer in intermittent fasting and is leery of short term lab rat studies and temporary fixes. He offers real world advice, to get real world results for real people who have jobs, families and other life commitments.

Bertherring.com

Megan Ramos worked with Dr. Fung for 16 years as a medical researcher. She is also a cofounder of Intensive Dietary Management.

Intensivedietarymanagement.com

Dr. Thomas N. Seyfried is a Boston College professor and award-winning writer who received several medals and commendations for his military service in Vietnam.

Mark Sisson founded Primal Kitchen, an organization that prepares healthy meals for delivery. Each meal has clean protein, healthy fats, and zero sugars. He has also authored two books, including a cookbook.

Robb Wolf authored *The Paleo Solution: The Original Human Diet*. He was a student of Professor Loren Cordain who wrote *The Paleo Diet*. He was a state powerlifting champion and amateur kickboxer who is co-owner of one of the nation's top 30 gyms, as ranked by *Men's Health* magazine.

Robbwolf.com

Chapter Summary

& Analysis

The Complete Guide to Fasting: Heal Your Body Through Intermittent, Alternate-Day, and Extended Fasting

Introduction

Jason Fung, MD

Dr. Fung loves to solve puzzles, and that's how he has come to be the expert of many topics, not the least of which is nutrition. Unfortunately, during nine years of medical school, he claims to have only spent no more than four hours on the topic, which is traditional. During his studies, he has made the following determinations:

- A low carb diet is better than low fat for losing weight

- A low carb diet is also better for cholesterol, blood sugar and blood pressure

But it still didn't make sense, because everything from the past leads us to believe that reduction of caloric intake is the best way to lose weight; however, that is wrong. What causes obesity is a hormonal imbalance, not caloric imbalance. Insulin is a fat storing hormone, so by reducing insulin in our bodies, we naturally lose weight.

So, for type 2 diabetes, the medical industry has been treating it with insulin to reduce sugar levels; however, adding insulin also adds weight. Our bodies have developed a natural resistance to insulin.

The question (or puzzle for Dr. Fung), is what causes insulin resistance?

Introduction

Jimmy Moore

Jimmy Moore, well known international author and co-author of this book once weighed 410 pounds and was highly skeptical of fasting practices. However, after following a low carb diet, Jimmy lost 180 pounds in one year and then he created an online platform: **Livin' La Vida Low Carb Show**.

Jimmy's experience started when he interviewed Boston College Professor Thomas L. Seyfried in 2009. The professor had been researching alternative cancer treatments and had evidence that an annual seven to ten-day water fast would help to prevent cancer.

Jimmy started fasting thanks to that interview.

First attempt: And Intermittent fast (IF) for 24 hours. He stopped eating around 6 p.m. and didn't eat again until after 6 pm the following day. It wasn't a great experience:

- Lack of caffeine led to a horrible headache

- His extreme hunger led him to overeat

- He tried to satisfy himself with diet sodas, which only enhanced his hunger

- He also found that he was not taking in enough salt

- A better option to the diet sodas would have been bone broth with sea salt

- He didn't try fasting again until 2011

His second attempt was better since he had learned from his earlier mistakes.

- This time, he didn't go a full 24 hours, rather he changed it to 18 to 24 hours and he did so for a full week.

- He stopped eating again around 6 pm each evening and then tried to make it until around 2 pm the following day before eating.

- This was great, as his impulse to eat ceased to exist

- He followed a ketogenic diet, which consists of low carbs, moderate protein, and high fat.

- Being in a state of ketosis teaches the body to burn fat first, then sugar. That is the opposite of the body's natural tendency.

- Still, a whole week without food was difficult, especially for the first three days.

- Days 4 and 5 were fabulous for him; he felt great

- And then days 6 and 7 were unpleasant, his blood sugar had plummeted to the 50s, had lost 13 pounds of mostly water weight.

- He had continued his usual exercise routine during the week.

- He was surprised that at the end of the week, his bowel movements were still typical, which shows how much waste our bodies hold.

- He had also continued with his usual nutritional supplements.

- He drank bone broth and added some bouillon cubes

- And now he had become a fat burner, not a sugar burner.

  Lessons learned: if you feel a need to eat, then eat. But, make sure you understand if your body is starving or if it's just your body expecting food at the customary meal time.

Next, Jimmy tried a three week or 21 days fast. He didn't make it to 21 days but was compelled to stop at 17 days, blaming added stress in his life at the time.

He lost 19 pounds, 16 of which stayed off after a month and many of his blood metrics were significantly reduced. Most of which are heart health indicators. For example:

- Cholesterol down 100 points

- LCL-C down 88 points

- HDL-C down 11 points (good cholesterol)

- Triglycerides down 22 points

- Insulin down 3.9 points

He finally tried a full 31 days fast and learned that the longer fasting periods were more successful for him.

- He paused his fast at day 13, day 16 and day 22 and made it to the full 31 days

- He lost 22.4 pounds, 14 of which stayed off

- Again, experienced noteworthy blood metric reductions

Jimmy is now a fasting fan and continues to experiment with fasting lengths and has a huge following on his *Livin' La Vida Low Carb Show.*

Chapter One

This chapter opens by explaining the difference between fasting, which is voluntary, and starving, which is involuntary. People experience starvation during wars and famine,, they are powerless to control hunger. Fasting can last as long or as short as you want, you fast every day between dinner and breakfast the next morning. You exercise full control over the timing as well as your intake to sustain your body's needs. Fasting is thousands of years old and has no defined standard duration; however, it has been forgotten as an option for weight loss. As a matter of fact, it is now viewed as something terrible.

The truth is we can fast! It has tremendously valuable health benefits.

Dr. Fung remembers growing up in the 1970s when we ate three meals a day, with no snacking in between meals. And obesity wasn't as much of an issue in those days. This information is supported by the National Health and Nutrition Examination Survey (NHANES). In addition, NHANES can report that today, we eat five to six times daily, which means our original fasting period between meals and at night is dramatically shortened. That isn't a good thing.

When we eat, our insulin goes up; sugar is stored in our liver, and so is fat. Conversely, when we fast, our insulin is decreased, thus burning our stored sugar and body fat. As we noted in Jimmy Moore's fasting experience, reaching ketosis means that the body has left the "fed state" and moved to the better "fasted state."

Five stages of metabolism: (all of which are natural and healthy)

- Feeding

- Post absorptive state

- Gluconeogenesis

- Ketosis

- Protein conservation

By regularly lowering our insulin levels, we are naturally improving our sensitivity to insulin. Our bodies become more responsive to insulin. Having a high insulin resistance is the root cause of type 2 diabetes, as well as other health ailments like blood pressure, obesity, stroke, etc. Lower insulin levels will also help reduce salt and water retention in our bodies. Electrolytes remain stable, adrenaline,metabolism, and growth hormones increase.

Fasting alone isn't the answer; we still need to maintain a healthy diet. The basic nutritional rules are:

- Eating more whole and unprocessed foods

- Less sugar and refined grains

- More natural fats

- Balance feeding with fasting

Fasting Success Story:
Samantha

Samantha was diagnosed with type 2 diabetes at the age of 37. She felt helpless and hopeless. Her doctor wasn't much help. After doing some Internet searching, she found Dr. Fung and began fasting three to five days per week. She was pleased with her results:

- Lost 30 pounds in four months

- Blood sugar consistently in the 70s

- Immediate improvement in the numbness in her feet and hands

- Blood pressure decreased

- She was able to get off her medications for this ailment

Chapter Two

Chapter two is about the history of fasting, which is as old as humankind. Several religions mandate some degree of fasting. For example, Buddhist Monks don't eat anything after twelve noon until the next morning. So, some people fast for spiritual reasons. Here are a few notable characters that believed in fasting:

- Hippocrates

- Plutarch

- Ancient Greeks believed fasting was good for cognitive and mental health

- Paracelsus

- Benjamin Franklin

- Mark Twain

Chapter Three

This chapter is devoted to busting six myths that are incorrectly considered truths:

- Fasting put you in starvation mode

- Fasting makes you burn muscle

- Fasting causes low blood sugar

- Fasting results in overeating

- Fasting deprives the body of nutrients

- It's just crazy

Dr. Fung, Jimmy Moore, and the fasting all-stars along with thousands of their followers have dis-proven each myth.

Chapter Four

Chapter four describes the advantages of fasting:

- It's simple

- It's free

- It's convenient

- You can enjoy life's little pleasures

- It's powerful

- It's flexible

- It works with any diet (diet alone is destined for failure)

Fasting Success Story:
Elizabeth

Elizabeth was diagnosed with type 2 diabetes in 2004 and she immediately went to a low carb, low-calorie diet and lost 66 pounds in 18 months. As the weight started coming back on, she realized that the diet was just not sustainable.

- In 2010, she was diagnosed with nonalcoholic fatty liver

- By 2011, she was taking 120 units of long acting insulin daily at bedtime, plus 80 units of rapid acting insulin three times a day with each meal.

- In 2015, she met Dr. Fung and began fasting three days per week. She lost 46 pounds and 31 inches from her waistline.

Chapter Five

The advice we've been given from experts for years has been to eat less and move more; however, that doesn't work. During the past 20 years this has been our mantra, yet over the same period, obesity rates have skyrocketed.

We all know of *The Biggest Loser* television show that has helped struggling dieters lose weight. During 30 weeks of filming, the average weight loss is 127 pounds. We tracked 14 contestants and 13 of them had regained all of their weight in six years or less. That's 93 percent failure because the life style there lived while filming was not sustainable in "real" life.

Insulin plays an essential role in weight loss. Low insulin levels allow our bodies to more readily get to fat cells and burn them. Lower insulin levels also trigger the burning of fat cells. The job of insulin is to move glucose from our bloodstream so it can be used for energy. When a body develops insulin resistance, it can no longer move the glucose and that's how our blood sugar levels build up. The body then develops a resistance to insulin.

When insulin levels remain consistently high, our body will continue to store fat cells for energy. On top of high insulin, we have always been taught to reduce our caloric intake, and the combination of both only further slows our metabolism.

Fasting is the solution to overcome this vicious cycle. Why not just remain on a low carb diet to keep insulin low? Because protein from animal sources will also increase insulin. And all that means is that fasting is a more robust solution than just keeping our carb intake low. Fasting will stop insulin resistance, lowering calories doesn't.

Avoiding intrusive bariatric surgery is an excellent reason to fast. The surgery is just a forced fast, and you end up on a ketogenic diet.

Cortisol is another hormone that naturally releases in times of stress, and fasting can be stressful. However, there is no evidence that fasting plays any role in cortisol levels.

While fasting will produce weight loss, the degree and the speed of loss will vary by individual. The key is persistence and patience!

Chapter Six

The World Health Organization just released its first global report on diabetes in 2016. Although the disease is thousands of years old, diabetes diagnosis has quadrupled since 1980.

Dr. Fung addresses how insulin has been responsive to type 1 diabetes versus type 2. Type 2 diabetes is not a prejudiced disease; it is impacting all genders, ages, ethnicities, and education levels. The age influenced by this disease is steadily getting younger and younger.

Today, diabetes is still considered a chronic and progressive disease; however, bariatric surgery disproves that theory. Diabetes often improves within just weeks of the surgery, so we do not believe the depressing diagnosis that many doctors communicate to their patients.

Dr. Fung describes why fasting is effective for type 2 diabetes with a great analogy about a train. Glucose molecules are passengers waiting to board an empty train. Insulin triggers the doors to open and the molecules march inside. But if the train is already full, the molecules can't get in and this is the beginning of insulin resistance. The insulin will continue to keep pushing harder to get the glucose into the blood stream until it eventually overflows.

How do we stop the madness? Two ways:

- Stop adding glucose to our bodies (low carb diet)

- Burn off excess glucose (via fasting)

If you are already on medications for type 2 diabetes, talk to your doctor before starting a fast. Careful and consistent monitoring is essential! Generally, we suggest no diabetes medications while fasting, but again, consult with your physician before you begin a fast.

Fasting Success Story: Megan

Megan was one of those envied people who could eat anything and everything and not gain an ounce. At least that was the case until she hit the age of 26 and packed on 53 pounds in four months. She was miserable and began restricting her calorie intake to 800 a day. She was also exercising for 60 minutes five days a week, but she wasn't losing weight. ARGGGGGG!!

She was eventually diagnosed as pre diabetic and also had a rare cancer. Having been in medical research since she was 18, she was acutely aware of the adverse impacts of type 2 diabetes. At the time, she was the research assistant to Dr. Fung who was in the process of developing his Intensive Dietary Management (IDM) Program. Although Megan was skeptical of fasting and struggled greatly during her first two weeks of a 24 hour fast. She fought through and became a believer in fasting. She knows when she needs to eat, versus when she wants to eat. She experienced headaches, nausea, and tremors, but was able to overcome those symptoms with bone broth and sea salt. On eating days, she would add a spoonful of coconut oil or avocados to help her feel full.

Fast forward three months: Megan is down 33 pounds and has reached her target weight. In another few months, she was down 60 pounds and maintaining that weight with ease for over 18 months. Even though she allows herself to indulge at times, she has successfully maintained her ideal weight to this day.

She shares a few thoughts on IDM and it's positive impacts on patients worldwide.

Chapter Seven

Fasting has other advantages like cell cleansing, fat burning, anti-aging, and neurological benefits. The severe caloric intake decrease naturally causes most of our organs to become smaller. The exception to that rule are brains, and for men, testicles. Even brain power is saved; fasting helps us retain an optimal level of intelligence and focus.

Further evidence of our brain power was again proven during World War II when American prisoners of war, who were severely starved, described the ability to recite entire books from memory. One even learned Norwegian in less than seven days.

Much like other mammals, when humans are full and satisfied, our brains tend to become foggier. When we become hungry, our mental capacity increases and is more innovative.

Fasting has proven itself to be beneficial to fighting Alzheimer's and Huntington disease. It improves memory and general brain activity.

We all know that with aging bodies, sometimes things don't work as well as they once did. It's just the natural process. Fasting helps to cleanse our bodies of toxins and cellular debris and contributes to growing new cells, which results in body rejuvenation.

Chapter Eight

We have been dancing around the fact that fasting also improves our heart health, and this section looks at some of the specifics. High cholesterol has been tied to increased risk of heart attacks and stroke. Luckily, fasting reduces cholesterol. Triglycerides are another leading indicator of a high risk of heart disease to the tune of 61 percent greater risk. Guess what? Low carb diets reduce triglycerides.

Conversely, diet has zero impact on cholesterol. Studies have repeatedly supported the fact that cholesterol, which is generated by our liver, can best be controlled via fasting.

Chapter Nine

You've heard the adage that "love hurts," and so does hunger! This chapter focuses on the nature of hunger and what it means. Generally, about four hours after our last meal, we feel hunger and believe it's time to eat. If that's true, a 24 hour fast would be impossible to successfully complete! We have trouble recognizing actual hunger pains as compared to our minds just telling us it's time to eat.

Over the years we have "learned" eating behavior. If you grew up in a home where snacks were readily available and you became used to enjoying one between every meal, you have unintentionally trained your brain to tell you it's time to eat, even when its not. But you can overcome that message, even if you have to do it slowly, one snack at a time. Some other examples of how we unintentionally condition our brains to include:

- We are at a movie theater, we must have popcorn, sodas, and candy

- It's halftime at the football game; we must have hot wings, chips, dip, meatballs, pigs in a blanket

- It's 3 pm and our afternoon slump has kicked in, we must have caffeine and a snack

- It's 8 am; we're on our way to work, must grab sausage, egg and cheese biscuit plus hash browns

And the list goes on and on. Intermittent fasting is a great way to defeat our conditioning. Start small, skip that afternoon snack and look forward to a healthy dinner. Give that a few days and then stop the morning snack between breakfast and lunch, abandon the bedtime snack, and slowly you will begin to learn when you are actually hungry. And at the very least you will find yourself returning to three meals a day and zero snacking. If you want to continue, increase your fasting periods by skipping a meal, then two, then try a full 24-hour period of fasting. You can do it! It may not be easy, so here are some tips that we hope will be helpful:

- Artificial sweeteners increase hunger

- Try to remove yourself from temptations of cooking or smelling good food, it won't always be this way, just until you get used to this new habit

- Only eat at the table, no computer snacks or television nibbling

- Replace a bad habit with a "less bad" habit

- If you feel deprived passing on your bedtime snack, replace it with a cup of herbal tea

Hunger comes and goes in waves. if you can ride out the tide, what you feel as hunger will go away and you'll forget about it all together. Set goals and increase them as you go along. Eventually, you can strive for a three to seven day fast. Listen to your hormonal signals and avoid known triggers for eating. Behavior modification works.

Fasting Success Story:
Darryl

Darryl was referred to Dr. Fung in 2015 and was 36 years old. He had been diagnosed with type 2 diabetes 11 years prior, had high blood pressure, high cholesterol and only one kidney. He was also experiencing lower back pain from his obese tummy, which was turning into crippling arthritis. At the time, he was taking 70 units of insulin daily.

We started on a low carb, high-fat diet with intermittent 24 fasting three times a week and got immediate results. Within two weeks, we stopped all insulin because his blood sugar was consistently in the normal range. He was no longer considered a person with diabetes!

Chapter Ten

While we've been touting all benefits of fasting, it isn't for everyone. You should avoid fasting under the following conditions:

- If you are malnourished or underweight

- Children under the age of 18

- If you are pregnant or breastfeeding

- If you suffer from anorexia

You should consult your doctor before beginning any fasting program, and if you have:

- Gout

- Are taking any medications

- Have diabetes

- Gastroesophageal reflux disease (GRD)

Remember that if you start feeling sick, it's okay to stop your fast!

Chapter Eleven

Types of fasting include:

- Many fasts allow for the ingestion of noncaloric beverages like tea, black coffee, and water – no sweeteners of any kind

- Water only fasts, where you only intake plain water

- Juice fasts results are not as good as others because fruit juices have so much sugar in them. Technically, this is not a real fast

- During fat fasts people only partake of pure fats like butter, coconut oil, and cream. This again is not an accurate fast.

Best fasting practices are:

- Stay hydrated

- You can add lemon, lime, berries, orange slices or cucumber to add flavor to your water

- No sweeteners

- Tea (green, black, oolong, herbal) no more than two teaspoons of cream can be added

- Coffee, either caffeinated or decaffeinated and no more than two teaspoons of cream

- Bone broth (beef, pork, chicken or fish) and veggies and fresh seasonings are permitted (a recommended recipe is included in the book)

Chapter Twelve

Chapter 12 takes a deeper dive into intermittent fasting. It means exactly what you think it means, periods of fasting between periods of eating.

Fasting periods can be short (less than 24 hours) or longer (greater than 24 hours). Fast can range from 12 hours to three or more months. There is no "best" length.

The shorter fasts are usually:

- Performed more frequently (longer fasts are 24 to 36 hours in length)

- Much easier to fit conveniently into work and family schedules

- You still eat daily

- 12-hour fasts run overnight, so you eat three meals only between 7 am and 7 pm and then fast until 7 am the following morning. This method will help you avoid insulin resistance, but may not result in weight loss.

- Using the same time example from above, you will stop eating at 7 pm and wait until 11 am the following day to eat again, so you're basically skipping breakfast. Weight loss will happen slow and steady with this method.

- 20-hour fasts tend to be more focused on what to eat, rather than the essential when to eat; they also mix in interval training for best results.

Circadian rhythms are predictable and repetitive cycles. They are highly tied to ambient light and the time of day or seasons. Studies on this phenomenon are few, but in one study conducted in 2013, two groups of overweight women both ate the same number of daily calories; one group had a big breakfast and the second group had a big dinner. The late dinner group had a larger rise in insulin and the big breakfast group lost more weight. So, this supports having your biggest meal earlier in the day. Hunger patterns also followed circadian rhythms.

Longer fasts are usually:

- Performed with less frequency

- Offer better results

- Can be harder to start

ɔnger fasting periods in more depth and

ɔ of longer fasts. Longer fasting periods

ısistently low insulin levels. When doing a long term fast, constant monitoring of metrics is critical. Fasting will lead to hunger pains; however, you should not feel sick. Stop the fast immediately if you feel bad and see your doctor.

Risks are a bit higher, but monitoring should help mitigation. Diabetic medication will need to be reduced on fasting days and should be discussed with your doctor.

• 24-hour fasts are best at the beginning because you still get one meal per day, which also lowers risk, and it's easy to fit into your life schedule as well. Don't limit your calories too much after the fast, but consistently stick to low carb, high fat, and unprocessed foods.

- The 5:2 diet, which was popularized by Dr. Michael Mosley is another viable option. In this instance, you eat normally for five days and limit calories on the remaining two days. On the limited days, women can eat up to 500 daily calories and men, up to 600.

- Alternate day fasting is akin to the 5:2 diet. You limit calorie intake every other day and eat regularly every other day. Another great way to ease into a fasting protocol.

- 36 hours fasting on the IDM program occurs three times per week for type 2diabetes patients. You eat your final meal around 7 pm on day one, fast all of day two, and eat one meal again on the morning of day three. This won't reverse your diabetes; however, it is enough to significantly reduce insulin in your body.

- 42-hour fasts allow you to enjoy dinner around 7 pm on day one, fast on day two and don't eat until after noon on day three.

Fasting Success Story:
Sunny and Cherrie

Sunny came into the IDM program on the maximum dose of daily Metformin plus 70 unit of daily insulin. He had gotten to this point over about a ten-year period. We put him on a 36 or 42 hour fast three days per week. He experienced amazing results quickly and felt well during the entire process. Between September 2015 and March 2016, Sunny's sugar had stabilized and he was classified as pre diabetic and was off of all sugar medications.

Sunny's younger sister Cherrie was impressed with her brother's results and had much of the same experience. She began on the IDM program in February 2016 and within two weeks, she was fully off all three sugar medications and was losing pounds and inches. Within a month, she was off ALL six of her medications. Like Sunny, Cherrie felt well during her journey.

Type 2 diabetes is clearly a dietary issue. These are typical results of many IDM participants.

Chapter Fourteen

Extended fasting is anything that exceeds 42 hours. Results of 46 patients on an extended 14 days fast, performed in 1968, yielded excellent results. Two of the patients asked to be readmitted for another 14-day period.

During the 14 days, they were only allowed water, tea and coffee and at discharge were encouraged to follow a 600 to 1,000 calorie diet. After the first 14 days, the average weight loss was 17.2 pounds, blood sugar levels dropped and the three patients who had diabetes were off all medication within two weeks. All patients reported a good feeling of well-being and euphoria. One patient dropped out and one experienced some nausea; otherwise, there is little and rare evidence that extended fasting is detrimental to our bodies.

Two to three-day fasts are usually not recommended. Patients report that the second day is the worst so extending that to a seven to fourteen day fast is more efficient and functional. In the IDM program, seven to fourteen days is the most recommended start because results are quicker and more significant, which keeps the patient motivated. Patients often report that the longer fast is just as easy/difficult as a shorter period. It's like the difference between doing a cannonball in the deep end of the pool as opposed to a slow walk from the shallow water.

Refeeding syndrome is more likely to occur with any fast that exceeds 14 days. It is rare because it only happens if the patient becomes malnourished. Refeeding can happen if the body becomes depleted of electrolytes. You can prevent refeeding by:

- Not making an extended fast water only, drink bone broth and take a daily multivitamin

- Do your regular activity routine during the fast as this will help maintain bones and muscles

Chapter Fifteen

Summary of the best fasting tips are:

- Change your fasting strategy based on your personal results

- Set reasonable goals and stay the course

- Stay hydrated and drink lots of water

- Keep busy so you won't dwell on thoughts of food

- Drink coffee; it has a mild appetite suppressant

- Ride out the hunger waves

- Don't tell people you're fasting; they will likely try to discourage you; however, a small support group could be of benefit

- Your first fasts will be difficult. Just give yourself 30 days and you will see and feel your body comfortably adjusting

- On non-fasting days, eat low carb and high natural fats

- Avoid bingeing

- Set a realistic fasting pattern that fits into your life's schedule

When you break your fast, these are the best snacks for you:

- A quarter to a third cup of pine nuts, almonds, macadamias or walnuts

- One table spoon of peanut or almond butter

- Cottage cheese or a small salad, with no dressing

- Small bowl of raw veggies drizzled with olive oil and vinegar

- A bowl of vegetable soup

- A small amount of meat (three slices of prosciutto or two slices of pork belly)

Also remember that when you bre

- Keep portions small

- Chew your food thoroughly

- Eat slowly

- Drink at least eight ounces of cold water before you end your fast and again after your first meal

...ommon concerns that some people experience ...clude:

Hunger

- Drink lots of water; green tea has high antioxidants

- Cinnamon is an appetite suppressant, add it to your tea or coffee

- Coffee helps to suppress hunger

- Chia seeds are high fiber and omega 3s

Dizziness means your blood pressure is too low or you are dehydrating

 Drink more water

 Add sea salt to your bone broth

Constipation is also expected as waste in your body lessens

- Add more fiber and fruit and veggies on non-fasting days

- Metamucil can be taken during or after fasting

- If you're not feeling discomfort, chances are it's all good

Heartburn can be avoided by keeping your meals small, and:

- Raise the head of your bed

- Add lemon to sparkling water

- Stay up for at least 30 minutes after eating

To combat muscle cramps, try:

- Take a magnesium supplement

- Soak in Epson Salt

- Use magnesium oil on your skin

This 15th and closing chapter ends with FAQs, problems to watch for, the Dawn phenomenon, and eating out. The bottom line here is: you need to figure out how fasting best fits into your lifestyle.

Part Three

This section offers you a number of resources including:

- Fasting fluid options

- Fasting Protocols for 24, 36 and 42 hours, seven to 14 days fasting periods

- Recipes

Recipes

Berry Parfait

Bulletproof Coffee

Essential Bone Broth

Grain Free Pancakes

Mini Frittatas

Simple Homemade Bacon

Grain Free Cauliflower Pizza

Chicken "Breaded" in Pork Rinds

Chicken Drumsticks Wrapped in Bacon

Chicken Stuffed Bell Peppers

Game Day Wings

Homemade Chicken Fingers

Steak Fajitas

Arugula and Prosciutto Salad

Pear and Arugula Salad with Pine Nuts

Strawberry and Kale Salad

Tomato, Cucumber and Avocado Salad

Avocado Fries

Discussion Questions

about

The Complete Guide to Fasting: Heal Your Body Through Intermittent, Alternate-Day, and Extended Fasting

1. Discuss starving versus fasting.

2. Discuss the benefits of fasting.

3. Bust five of the six myths associated with fasting.

4. What is refeeding syndrome and what are the two recommended steps to prevent it from occurring?

5. Discuss the various short-term fasts and their implications.

6. Discuss the successes associated with IDM

7. Who should not participate in a fast?

8. Discuss the fasting tips and what you add to the list.

9. Discuss some of the primary concerns associated with starting a fast.

10. When and why would you want to use a short term fast versus an extended fast?

Publication/Author Information

about

The Complete Guide to Fasting: Heal

Your Body Through Intermittent,

Alternate-Day, and Extended Fasting

You can usually find Dr. Jason Frederick Fung, MD in Oakland, CA. Born in 1974, he is a Dermatologist with 18 years of experience. He is a 1999 graduate of the University of Rochester School of Medicine and Dentistry and his residency was fulfilled at Barnes Jewish Hospital. Dr. Fung is affiliated with Alta Bates Summit Medical Center Alta Bates Campus.

While his specialty is dermatology, he also has expertise in:

- Acne Vulgaris
- Acne Rosacea
- Actinic Keratosis
- Basal Cell
- Excision
- Melanoma
- Mole
- Psoriasis
- Rash
- Rosacea
- Skin Biopsy
- Skin Cancer

Dr. Fung is also the recipient of several awards including:

- Compassionate Doctor Recognition
- On-Time Doctor Award
- Patients' Choice Award
- Patients' Choice 5th Anniversary Award

When Dr. Fung is not in Oakland, you may find him in Toronto, Canada. He finished medical school at the University of Toronto, followed by a fellowship at the University of California, Los Angeles at the Cedars Sinai Hospital with a specialty in nephrology. He has also been affiliated with the Scarborough General Hospital since 2001.

The good doctor also founded the Intensive Dietary Management (IDM) program in Toronto, Canada. Today he still serves as Medical Director. The IDM program focuses on:

- Obesity
- High Blood Pressure
- Fatty Liver
- Diabetes
- High Cholesterol
- Cancer

- Alzheimer's Disease

Dr. Fung's co-author on this book was Jason W. Moore who is an associate professor of Sociology at Binghamton University. He has written many books on topics including history, historical geography, and capitalism. He is also a recipient of several international awards.

Other Books

by

Jason Fung, MD and Jimmy Moore

The Obesity Code: Unlocking the Secrets of Weight Loss

Keto Clarity: Your Definitive Guide to the Benefits of a Low Carb, High Fat Diet

Cholesterol Clarity: What the HDL is Wrong with my Numbers?

Ketogenic Cookbook: Nutritious Low Carb, High Fat Paleo Meals to Heal Your Body

So - what did you think?

Brief Books pledges to always do our very best to produce high quality and entertaining books for you to enjoy. With that being said - the opinions, comments, criticisms, and compliments that we receive from fellow readers are always being taken to heart.

Take part to keep us going, add your review on Amazon and tell us and others what you think!

Thanks once again.

Sincerely,

Brief Books

Made in the USA
Lexington, KY
30 January 2018